A PROPER INSTITUTION

A Twentieth Century Fund Paper

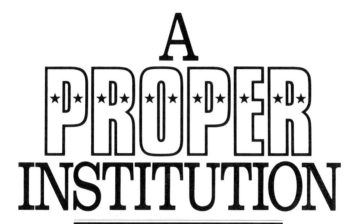

A PROPER INSTITUTION

GUARANTEEING TELEVISED PRESIDENTIAL DEBATES

By John B. Anderson

Priority Press Publications/New York/1988

Library of Congress Cataloging-in-Publication Data

Anderson, John Bayard, 1922–
  A proper institution.

  "A Twentieth Century Fund paper."
  Bibliography: p.
  Includes index.
  1. Presidents—United States—Election.
2. Campaign debates—United States. 3. Television in politics—United States. I. Title.
JK524.A76 1988   324.7'3'0973   88-31817
ISBN 0-87078-253-3
ISBN 0-87078-252-5 (pbk.)

Foreword

Since the historic debate between John F. Kennedy and Richard M. Nixon was aired in the fall of 1960, televised debates between the major candidates have emerged as a central event in presidential campaigns. Not only have the debates become one of the few forums where the candidates actually confront one another, but they are generally acknowledged to carry substantial weight with the electorate. Nevertheless many decry their stylized quality, their lack of substance.

The Twentieth Century Fund has long been involved in the debate about debates. Over the years, the Fund has, in various publications— *Voters' Time, With the Nation Watching,* and *Beyond Debates*—as well as in informal conferences, pushed for making a series of presidential (and vice presidential) debates a permanent feature of American political life. Most recently, with the paper *For Great Debates* by Newton N. Minow and Clifford M. Sloan, the Fund played a role in setting up the Commission on Presidential Debates, which sponsored this political season's round of debates.

The Fund's interest in the debates was shaped for nearly twenty years by Murray J. Rossant, its director. Never one to be satisfied with his or the Fund's efforts, he commissioned, during the last year of his life, another paper on the debates from John B. Anderson. As a U.S. congressman for many years and candidate for the presidency in 1980, Mr. Anderson has had a privileged position from which to observe the campaign process. It is likely that his proposals for reforming the debates will strike many observers as provocative, even radical; it is certain that they will accomplish what Murray set out to do: inspire debate.

Marcia Bystryn, ACTING DIRECTOR
The Twentieth Century Fund
October 1988

Contents

Chapter 1
The Need for Reform

One major American contribution to the annals of politics is the concept of workable consensual government: we have created a system of government, as the great political statements of our national history affirm, to operate at the behest of the governed, and by their consent.

When it is not practical to obtain this consent directly (as in a small town meeting, for example), Americans have used representatives to be the medium of consent.

But for representative government to be truly based on consent, the representatives must be fully *accountable* to their constituents; without accountability, they effectively become "rulers" in an authoritarian sense. The heart of representative democracy, therefore, is accountability, and the quality of the bond between us and our representatives is a good measure of the quality of democracy: it defines how "democratic" government actually is.

Few Americans, on the surface at any rate, would disagree with these observations, but we must recognize that theory and practice have often diverged, especially in recent times.

There are several theories of representation in our political tradition, none of which captures the full flavor of our consensual system, but all of which, taken together, reflect the mix of attitudes about the role of representatives, including the president:[1]

• Representatives can be viewed as *delegates* sent with close instruction by the voters to represent them. In this view, the role of representatives is to monitor voter opinion carefully and to reflect it as accurately as possible.

• Representatives can be viewed as *agents,* hired by the electorate to represent them as one might hire an attorney to represent a client. In this case, representatives, while attentive to the interests of their constituencies, would be expected to use their independent judgment as to how best to represent their client's interests, in this case the voter.

• Representatives can be thought of as people of intrinsic quality or merit selected by the voter for the very purpose of exercising independent judgment in most or all matters. This is the model of representation made famous by Edmund Burke in his speech to the electors of Bristol and made heroic by John F. Kennedy in his *Profiles in Courage.* Such people can be considered truly representative because the voters trust them to behave in an honorable and thoughtful manner; they expect them to put the national interest ahead of short-term expediencies.

These people are "representatives" because the voters consent to be represented by them by voting them into office. They are held accountable (in democratic theory) by the *public explication and justification* of their actions, even if those actions might be counter to their current opinion of their constituents. (It is this willingness to assume public responsibility, either when the actions are taking place or after the fact, that distinguishes the accountable actions of a Burke from the nonaccountable actions of an Oliver North.) Such representatives have been called *trustees.*

Although these models of representation were originally applied primarily to legislators who wrote laws, acting in the name and in the stead of the people whom they represented, these concepts of representation, especially the trustee concept, can also apply to the president and vice president: by selecting our civil executive leaders, we are a representative Republic as well as a representative Democracy.

Given the size, influence, and permanence of the federal bureaucracy, however, and its tendency to seek autonomy and independence from external supervision, there is always a danger in any modern society that bureaucratic government will replace democratic government.

Congress, to be sure, plays a major oversight role in supervising the administration of government, and statutory accountability is the hallmark of enabling legislation. Congress, therefore, attempts to bring bureaucracy into the ambit of popular accountability. But the president's role is more fundamental because he and his appointees are directly responsible for governmental conduct in the most immediate sense. He is the person primarily responsible for the conduct of federal administration.

For the "permanent government"—as it has been aptly called by the Tower Commission—to be fully accountable, even in theory, to the public which it is supposed to serve, two conditions must obtain: (1) the appointed officials of government must be accountable to the elected officials—notably to the president but also to the Congress and (2) the elected officials must be fully accountable to the public. Otherwise you do not have a representative or democratic form of government.

The apparent recent breakdown in the first of these conditions is beyond the scope of this study. This breakdown was given dramatic witness by the Iran-Contra scandal, and became the proper subject of examination by the Tower Commission and by a congressional joint committee during the summer of 1987. Much more still needs to be said, but it will not be said here.

The breakdown of the second condition *is* a concern of this study: are the president and the chief officers of government being held fully accountable to the public for their actions, and if not, what can be done about this? More specifically, can the election process itself—and especially the presidential debate—be used to increase accountability?

There are several ways in which Americans traditionally have held their public offices accountable. One is to demand a public review of their action: the Constitution, for example, requires Congress to keep a journal of its proceedings and mandates the president publicly to state reasons for vetoing acts of Congress. The original rationale behind the State of the Union Address was also, in part, to require the president to give an annual public accounting to the Congress.

A second tradition of accountability has been grounded in an adversary process in which officials are required to justify their (intended and actual) actions through a process of cross-examination. Examples of this include the explicit adversarial dimensions of congressional debates and the implicit adversarial dimensions found in congressional hearings.

The somewhat uncertain tradition of presidential press conferences is viewed by many as being part of an adversarial process at work, but the legitimacy of the press's role as adversary to the president (as opposed to being merely an elicitor of information) has never been universally accepted by Americans, and its constitutional role, if any, has never been established.

The most important tradition of accountability, of course, its ultimate dimension in the United States, is the election. Theoretically, at least, the "ballot box" forces a public "accounting" of past action (or establishes a record of intent for the future) and provides a forum for adversarial cross-examination of past records and future proposals. It provides for the systematic and periodic direct approval or disapproval of representative conduct.

Elections legitimize governmental conduct in a way no other system can: we respect our government, participate creatively (not destructively) in society, and obey the laws because we, as Americans and as individuals with rights prior to the laws, have consented to their enactment *and* administration through a process of representation that embodies accountability.

The quality of the election campaign, therefore, reflects the degree to which a country is actually a representative democracy.

Elections, however, are more than just vehicles for legitimizing government; they serve a pragmatic function as well. It is implicit in our democratic faith that elections are a good way of *selecting* qualified agents to represent us as well as *legitimizing* their conduct. It is a process of getting the leaders we deserve because we are the ones who picked them, presumably based on our good judgment in determining the qualifications of aspirants to public office. Americans have traditionally believed that the democratic process of selecting leadership is not only the most just, but also the most effective—voters expect elections to help produce both accountability in officials and quality in government. There is, however, a widespread view today that we are getting neither. And the catalog of complaint is a long one. There are some major areas of concern.

To begin with, the system of holding incumbent presidents accountable for their actions has broken down. Presidential staffs have become even less accountable. This is not only the result of the "imperial presidency" phenomenon of increasing presidential isolation but also a result of there being no effective forums in which to hold the president and all his "men" accountable:

• The presidential press conference has become a sporadic exercise in mutual manipulation, in which reporters try to entrap the president into saying something sensational, and the president tries to trap the press into becoming a sounding board against which he can score publicity points with well-chosen one-liners. It is hardly a source of quality information; it is certainly not a means of holding the president accountable for his policies or for those of his staff in any systematic way.

• The congressional hearing, while theoretically still a powerful vehicle of accountability is also fast becoming an exercise in mutual manipulation and petty demagoguery. The hearings can, and to some extent do, provide for a systematic review of policy, but the president himself does not defend his policies in this forum. In this respect, executive accountability to the legislature is fragmented and, at the second tier of government, in sharp contrast to the practice in Britain, Canada, and most other Western democracies where the head of government must defend the whole range of government policies against the opposition in direct and open debate before the legislature.

• The State of the Union Address, originally designed to be a vehicle of presidential accountability to the Congress and the public, has become largely a media event—an exercise in rhetoric with very little hard content. The televised opposition responses to the State of the Union, lacking the majestic forum that the joint session of Congress provides to the president, start off in a visually inferior context and are often delivered by speakers of uneven quality. To date, the responses have not been used as effective means of holding presidents accountable for their policies.

• The periodic televised presidential policy speech, despite the practice of having press commentary and opposition response following it, is almost entirely the president's show. The speeches are delivered on topics and at times of the president's own choosing and usually in a visually favorable context. Again, there is no forensic equality in the dialogue between the president and his respondents; in fact, many observers question the legitimacy of an unelected press acting as critical commentator following these broadcasts.

To be sure, plenty of public criticism is still printed and aired in this country. Editorials are written, and some people will read them. More to the point, many politicians respond to printed criticism as if it had a wider audience than it actually does. In addition, some television journalism is of high quality and adversarial in nature—for example, "Nightline," "60 Minutes," "20/20," "Meet the Press," and "Face the Nation." Since these are some of the top-rated shows in America, it is clear that good television journalism is of interest to viewers.

However, these shows, like congressional hearings, do not give us a systematic forum in which the president can be forced to take responsibility for the policies of his administration or pledge action for which he and his party can be held accountable in the future.

As far as the regular news programs themselves are concerned, the ability of the White House to set the news agenda, through both statement and deliberate action, seems to have grown dramatically during the past decades to the point where an increasing percentage of coverage on the evening news seems to be government inspired, if not almost government directed. The evolution of the modern presidency has perhaps made this inevitable. In this context, views in opposition to those of the government are not adequately presented. With the government more often than not setting the agenda, critics are usually put in negative defensive positions where they must respond to government initiatives or literally take to the streets to create a visual (but not necessarily attractive) expression of their views.

The contemporary presidential campaign is also failing to fulfill adequately its two principal democratic objectives: giving the voter valid information on which to make electoral choices and creating a record of commitment for the purpose of future accountability. The failure is not total: campaigns still serve to hold administrations accountable (to some degree) for their actions, and they do provide voters with some information about the candidates. But they do not do their jobs as well as they could, and it seems that they are doing a worse job than they used to.

Presidential campaigns are structured less and less around policy choices and more and more around personality and image. To be sure, the character and competence of candidates comprise legitimate information that the voter should have, but it is not the only information. We also have a right to know where a candidate stands on issues (beyond a vague level of generality) and, more important, whether or not a candidate is competent to deal with these issues and to solve problems. Unfortunately, campaigns are not structured to force candidates to grapple with policy questions, nor are they structured to force candidates to offer solutions to our mounting domestic and foreign problems.

In the age of image makers and their thirty-second spots, this information is often hard to obtain. The contemporary campaign is a contrived affair—composed largely of pseudoevents artfully designed to create visuals for the evening news, symbolic visits to airports to claim a geographic presence in order to obtain media market exposure, and constantly repeated "stump speeches" carefully crafted for their rhetorical impact rather than for their policy content. The contemporary campaign is dominated by imagemakers and public relations experts, not by idea people and policy experts. This balance of power within the campaign has translated itself into a similar balance on the White House Staff.

Campaigns are designed neither to force candidates to recruit competent, policy-oriented staff around which to build an administration, nor to give evidence of their ability to do so, nor to present examples of the type of people who will serve in their administration, nor to expose such potential staff to voter scrutiny. In an age where the voter, as a practical matter, is selecting an administrative team as much as an individual candidate to run the government, such shortcomings are serious.

This is not a call for "responsible parties" or for some sort of blueprint democracy where candidates are required to develop detailed answers to detailed questions and then be expected to carry out their projects to the last letter.[2] Presidential candidates cannot, as a practical matter, be held to such a standard of conduct in the face of changing times and circumstances. But if it is unreasonable to ask candidates to present a specific solution to every problem, it is not unreasonable to make them demonstrate that they and their staffs do have the *ability to find* solutions. This is not happening today.

The role of the media in covering the presidential campaigns has contributed to these shortcomings. Walter Lippmann in 1922 wrote in a chapter entitled "The World Outside and the Pictures in Our Heads" that it is the mass media which create those pictures of what we really think about.[3] And a half century later, Theodore White wrote that the "power of the press in America is a primordial one. It sets the agenda of public discussion; and this sweeping political power is unrestrained by any law. It determines what people will talk and think about—an authority that in other nations is reserved for tyrants, priests, parties, and mandarins."[4] This power is today being exercised in a damaging way.

Although there are many responsible journalists who do cover the serious aspects of a campaign, a disproportionate amount of media coverage, and especially television coverage, is given to the candidate's political strategy to win the election and not to questions of policy content or the candidates' administrative abilities, judgment, and capacity to recruit and coordinate quality staff.

The contemporary journalistic instinct—and, again, television is the chief offender—is to cover events, not ideas, or, if covering ideas, to do so symbolically with little attention to content.[5] With the use of symbols, we are approaching the media "ideal" of a content-free campaign. A fascinating recent example of this—although the campaign involved should not be singled out for special opprobrium—was Senator Gary Hart's candidacy structured around the theme "A Campaign of New Ideas," which constantly repeated the need for new ideas while offering an extremely modest menu of innovative policy changes.

There are many examples of the tendency to cover events at the expense of ideas. One good illustration of this is the television news practice of covering a speech simply as a visual with a voice-over describing the event, with hardly any (or even no) audio coverage of the actual words of the speaker. This "event orientation" is the reason why the pseudoevent staged for the camera has become such an important part of the modern presidential campaign. It is also the ethos that is largely responsible for the tendency of the media to cover elections more like horse races than like serious exercises in democratic choice. This phenomenon will have important consequences for public policy.

There is no better example of this "event orientation" than media coverage of presidential debates. To begin, there is the season of covering the negotiations over whether or not there will be any debates, and, if so, how many and where. Then there is a phase of covering negotiations over the ground rules. After that, there is the coverage of the strategic preparation: What are the media experts advising? What are the managers doing? What is their image strategy? What are the candidates' forensic strengths and weaknesses? How are the candidates preparing for the debate? Are they conducting trial runs? Who is playing the opposition candidate(s) in the dress rehearsal? Are they practicing their opening and closing statements? How are they going to handle certain types of questions? What attention is being given to their dress, makeup, and other dimensions of their physical appearance?

With the public inundated by detailed speculations such as these and with coverage focused on style and strategy, the media create an ambience that tends to delegitimize, in advance, the policy relevance of the presidential debate. After the fact, television commentary is almost exclusively devoted to the question of who won and why, and not to the actual policy content of what was said: How did the candidates look? Did someone make an error? Did someone look strong? Did someone look tired and weak? Do the polls reveal a winner? What was the impact of the debates on the trial heat standings? What was their impact on the overall strategic position of the candidates in the campaign?

If any parts of the debate itself are replayed in subsequent coverage, they are the parts deemed by the media to have been the "events" (especially any gaffes) and not the messages (or ideas, if any) that the candidates were trying to set forth.

Another area for concern is the serious decline in the quality of public discourse on political questions. In many ways, this is the most fundamental problem we face in electoral politics. It is a truism that the quality of government and the quality of decisions made by government in a democracy can be no higher than the quality of public discourse in which the business of government is transacted. In fact, the quality of public discourse is a good guide to the quality of democracy: if public debate is conducted in language that is descriptively accurate, rich in content, and designed to provide practical information, then public choice can be sober and rational. Under such conditions, it is meaningful to talk in terms of democratic government.

Democracy assumes both an informed electorate and an open discussion of the great questions of the moment in understandable language that accurately reflects reality. But if public discourse is largely rhetorical in content, divorced from reality, and designed primarily to manipulate, then democracy cannot function well at all. Indeed, as George Orwell wrote, one of the greatest distinguishing features between democratic and authoritarian regimes is the nature and purpose of their public language. Deceptive language is a cornerstone of totalitarianism, and the ability to control and structure discourse is, perhaps, the single most important source of power that such a regime employs against its citizens.

Democratic government, as John Locke reminds us, based on a fair degree of trust between governors and governed, is impossible in the absence of a language whose meaning is agreed upon by the participants to the discourse. Trust and democratic government both depend upon honest communication.

So does freedom. For a people to be free, they must be informed. The essence of our political freedom is the ability to make informed choices, and these, in turn, depend upon the quality as well as the quantity of the information to which we have access. The quality of political discourse, therefore, is a measure of our freedom as well as a measure of the quality of our representative democracy.

It is difficult to avoid the conclusion that the quality of American public discourse has declined in recent decades. It is truly sobering to compare the stylistic quality and level of content of what is being said today in the conduct of public debate with the quality and content of public political utterances of the past. For example:

- Compare the level of policy content in Washington's Farewell Address to that of *any* speech of Johnson, Nixon, Carter, or Reagan.

- Compare the level of analysis and amount of policy content in the Federalist Papers to that of any current advocacy prose. The Federalist Papers, written as part of the public discourse of the late eighteenth century, were published in a newspaper and were designed to persuade the public to vote in a certain way. Today's editorials pale in comparison.

The language and level of conceptualization contained in the Federalist Papers were probably representative of the discourse that occurred at Philadelphia during the framing of the Constitution, and in the early Congresses of the United States. It was not a mere exercise in fancy rhetoric, although the language was polite. The concerns and the issues, however, were real; the level of analysis was high; the concepts, while sophisticated, were presented in understandable language. The intent was to persuade, but the appeal was to reason and to prudent reality, not to emotion and certainly not to fantasy.

- Compare the first inaugural address of Thomas Jefferson to the inaugural addresses of the second half of the twentieth century—even John Kennedy ruefully admitted that Jefferson's was much better than his own.

• Compare the language and level of analysis of the Lincoln-Douglas debates with those of the Carter-Ford or Reagan-Mondale debates. We sometimes forget that the Lincoln-Douglas debates were conducted between two hard-headed politicians running for office and attempting to defeat each other in the course of an election campaign. These were campaign debates. Again, here were real issues, fundamental issues of public policy, being debated in front of supposedly ignorant farmers and half-literate small-town merchants. And yet the level of discourse was certainly superior to that conducted today in front of audiences, one third of whose members have a college degree. And it would be hard to argue that the nineteenth-century audiences who heard those debates—or read the verbatim short-hand transcripts of them—failed to get their message.

There are plenty of other examples—the eloquent speeches of William Jennings Bryan and Woodrow Wilson, the emotional, yet content-laden orations of Theodore Roosevelt, the sharply contrasting political philosophies set forth in cogent detail by Herbert Hoover and Franklin Roosevelt in the 1932 campaign.

Indeed, the language of Harry Truman, although seldom eloquent, never failed to convey with great precision his concrete position on almost any issue of the day: you knew where he stood. And in 1952, we were treated to an election contest between an eloquent midwestern governor of extraordinary linguistic skill and a war hero (and incidentally, former speech writer) whose simpler language was nevertheless direct, filled with content, and quite clear.

The point is not that the linguistic skills of our earlier politicians were intrinsically superior to those of today or that our ancestors were more intelligent than our contemporaries. Nor is this a call for highly sophisticated, esoteric discourse understandable to only a few. It is a call for real issues to be debated realistically. It is a call for accuracy and content—aspects of discourse that the past contained and that the discourse of the present lacks.

How can we restore accountability in the political process? How can we make elections more meaningful? How can we force candidates to pay more attention to policy solutions? How can we induce the media to address their democratic responsibilities in a better way? How can we raise the level of public discourse on political questions? What can we do to make our government more representative?

Simply appealing to candidates (or to the press) to talk intelligently or to act responsibly is an exercise in wishful thinking. Moral suasion should not be dismissed entirely, but it is no match for the seeming imperatives shaped by the dynamics of modern campaigning that have brought us to where we are.

Change, however, is possible. The proposals contained in this report are suggestions for reforming one aspect of our presidential election campaign: the presidential debate process.

The evidence is that debates—even in their current mode—do have an impact on the political process: Philip Converse back in the 1960s concluded that voters who missed the Kennedy-Nixon debates exhibited the highest stability in voter intentions over the course of the campaign.[6] Debates are needed to energize the voters, to get them interested in the political process, not as entertainment, but as demonstrations that real problems are taken seriously by the politician and that it really does make a difference who wins an election.

Chapter 2
Process and Outcome

Proposals to reform the system by which we select our president should have two objectives: to improve the legitimacy of the process and to improve the quality of the result. The suggestions set forth in the detailed proposal presented later in this book are aimed at achieving these goals, as well as the related objective of improving the accountability of the president, once elected.

The legitimacy of the electoral process can be strengthened by forcing candidates to give voters more information about national issues, problems, and solutions—so voters can make more-informed decisions and can hold candidates more accountable in the future.

The accountability of presidents can be increased, both by forcing them to defend their policies in public forums and by giving the opposition greater opportunity to counter presidential initiatives with alternative suggestions.

The framers of the Constitution were concerned not only with the legitimacy of our political institutions and the legitimacy of the acts of government but also with the quality of government: How efficiently would government work? Would it serve the long-term as well as the short-term needs of the people? These concerns reflect the concerns about legitimacy: in a fundamental sense, governments that work well in the eyes of the people contribute to their own legitimacy.

If concern for representational legitimacy is the *democratic* dimension of our constitutional government, concern for institutions is our *republican* dimension. Indeed, the most fundamental difference both in principle and practice between a democracy and a republic is found in the different emphasis given to the importance of institutions: a democracy directly reflects the will of the people; a republic is based on the assumption that institutions can and should be used to shape the outcomes of the political process in predictably desirable ways.

It was their belief in the importance of lasting institutions that made the Founding Fathers republicans as well as democrats. They designed our institutions to make government both effective and nontyrannical. The system of checks-and-balances is the clearest example of institutions designed to shape outcome, but there are many others, including the Electoral College.

The original idea behind the Electoral College was to set a collection of "wise" electors between the voter and the ultimate choice. Electors were supposed to infuse their judgment into the process of presidential selection, to counterbalance the so-called whims of the electorate. In this respect, both democratic and republican tendencies were accommodated: the people chose the electors directly, but the electors acted as representatives who exercised their independent judgment.

The Electoral College has not, however, worked as it was intended. In fact, after the selection of George Washington, electors acted as delegates or agents under close instruction from the voters or, more accurately, from their parties.

But the spirit of the Electoral College—the concept that wise individuals should have input to the process of selecting the president—has lived on, specifically in the process by which candidates are *nominated* for president. In the early years of the Republic, congressional caucuses— a very select group—named their parties' candidates for president and narrowed the people's range of choice to two or (in the Era of Good Feeling) even one candidate.

In the 1830s and 1840s, a revolt against the influence of Washington insiders led to the invention of the national nominating convention. Again, the "wise individual" tradition continued—this time in the person of state party leaders. These individuals gathered in convention; negotiated the clash of interest groups; usually screened out the potential charlatans, demagogues, and embarrassments; and named candidates they thought had a reasonable chance to win the election.

In the past three decades, the process has changed again. The voter now has a much more direct role in naming the presidential candidates, and the concept of "wise individuals" determining the nomination of candidates has eroded (although the "superdelegate" rule in the Democratic party shows that it has not altogether disappeared).

As the deliberations of the "wise" have been replaced by the voice of the people, however, much thought has been given by the "wise" to the institutions through which people make known their choices. These institutions, as well as the rules of procedure, provide the strategic environment in which the nominating contests are fought and often decisively shape the outcome. That this has been recognized by both parties, but especially by the Democrats, is evident from the parade of reform commissions and rules changes that are regularly recommended.

Although the language of reform has been the language of justice and fairness, the process of reform has been a process of attempting to manipulate the outcome in ways advantageous to the factions proposing the reform measures.

Political parties clearly pay attention to their internal procedures—that is, how they produce candidates—but devote much less attention to the overall process of how the country produces a president and a government. The main concern of the parties is to win the election, not to question whether or not the result is good for the country, however sincere they may be in equating the two.[1]

The old system of convention choice was partly elitist, in that a small group of people selected the candidates. The current system, in its openness, is still partly elitist, in the sense that there is a *screening* process (rather than a *selection* process) in which groups (such as the press) play significant roles. What does the current system, including both the nominating and general election process, screen and test for?

1. The current process, with the Iowa caucuses and the New Hampshire primary, exposes candidates to extensive experience with retail politics: candidates must meet voters in small settings open to the public, talk to them, hear their problems and concerns, and be judged by them. It provides a vehicle to screen for the ability to relate to people firsthand in a small-group context.

2. The current process screens for recruitment and organizational skills: a candidate's ability to find people who can create a political organization, master logistics, and raise money.

3. The current process screens for strategic skills: the ability to engage in a strategic contest with strategically minded antagonists.

4. The current process, through its extensive primary season, screens out those with merely local or regional appeal.

5. The current process screens for character flaws by subjecting candidates to a thorough examination of their personal past—a screening process conducted by the media, the opposition, and other interested parties—that exposes them to ruthless public scrutiny.

6. The current process screens for the ability to stand pressure and intense public exposure.

7. The current process tests the ability of a candidate to communicate his or her views to the public and to develop media skills.

8. The current process forces a candidate to define his or her relationship to constituencies or interest groups.

9. The current process sometimes screens for a minimum level of policy awareness, in that the press may publicize serious flaws in a candidate's policies.

10. The current process, through survey research, also helps to identify the major worries and concerns of the voters.

The current system, therefore, forces candidates to develop organizational, strategic, and especially communication skills. What the current process does not do is:

1. Screen for candidates who can develop and defend detailed issue positions;

2. Screen for candidates who can demonstrate the administrative skills necessary to preside over the federal government;

3. Screen for candidates who can develop solutions to pressing policy needs;

4. Screen for candidates who can recruit and build a staff of policy experts to advise them as president;

5. Screen for candidates who can bring people together as a team and work as a team in an administration;

6. Screen for candidates who can find the people who can understand, relate to, and eventually master the permanent government in Washington.

In short, the process does not adequately screen for people who can confront policy choices, develop solutions, and run the government.[2]

We need a system that will either screen for these skills or *force candidates to develop them.* The suggestions set forth in this proposal, if adopted, would be a modest first step to help remedy some of these deficiencies.

Chapter 3
The Proposal in Brief

The essence of the proposal on presidential debates is to extend dramatically their scope and number (starting in 1992), make the receipt of federal election funds conditional on participation by the candidates, and structure them in such a way that the candidates are forced: (1) to develop specific policy positions; (2) to recruit competent policy advisors in advance of the election; and (3) to engage in substantive policy discourse.*

In addition, the proposal suggests that there be a new forum in which presidents must defend their administration's record in detail during the fall of the off-year congressional elections. The purpose would be to forge a link between the actions of the executive branch and the development of issues in the mid-term congressional elections.

Finally, suggestions are put forth to encourage public discussion of policy choices in advance of the fall campaign and in preparation for the debate season. These include an extensive schedule of open forums, debates between people who are not candidates but have achieved stature and wide recognition because of their identification with important and controversial issues. For example, former Commerce Secretary Peter G. Peterson has written and spoken extensively on the deficit issue; one

---

* The proposal is spelled out in detail in the next chapter.

of his proposals is "diet Colas," that is, putting limits on annual cost of living adjustments (COLAs). The head of the American Association of Retired Persons (AARP) would take a dramatically opposed position. Also, there would be a series of "platform defenses" in which representatives of the candidates are required to defend the specific planks of the platform.

The purpose of the reforms, in part, is:

- To improve the representative nature of our democracy by holding presidents, those who seek to be president, and their staffs more accountable both to the voter at large and to the various constituencies they represent;
- To raise the level of public discourse;
- To generate discussion of *solutions* to pressing problems;
- To force candidates and their staffs to demonstrate issue competence and problem-solving ability; and
- To provide voters with more information about the abilities of candidates and their staffs.

To coordinate all this public activity, I propose creation of a National Endowment for Presidential Debates, modeled on the pattern of the Corporation for Public Broadcasting. A set of fairly strict eligibility requirements would be set forth to restrict participation by nonmajor party candidates to "serious" ones, eliminating marginal or frivolous prospects.

More specifically, the proposal calls for creation of an intense fall schedule of twelve presidential and vice presidential debates and "issue conferences," six to be shown on network television and the rest (to avoid saturation) on PBS and cable. They would be arranged in the following chronological order:

1. An "agenda-setting" kickoff debate on network television during Labor Day week, featuring long opening and closing statements to give the candidates the opportunity to set their agendas for the campaign. The question format would resemble that of past presidential debates; the interrogators would be from the media.

2. Four sets of "issue conferences," each devoted to a specific policy area (such as arms control), with a single candidate *and his or her*

advisors. The participants would be questioned by policy experts, with follow-up questions and commentary by the interrogators. There would be one conference for each candidate, on the same issue, broadcast on cable and PBS on the same evening. These conferences (whose audience might be only a few million but would include those most interested in and familiar with the topic under discussion) would force the candidates to think seriously about policy choices, about recruiting the best advisors (who would also be subject to scrutiny), and about alternative solutions to the problems under consideration.

3. Three candidate/staff debates, again devoted to a specific policy area, in which the candidates, assisted by two or three experts, would be grilled by specialists in that policy area. This format would take the issue conference idea and raise it to the level of a full debate. It would force candidates and their selected experts to engage in substantive policy-oriented discourse. One of the three debates would be broadcast on network television, as detailed below, the others on cable and PBS.

4. A debate between the vice presidential candidates, following a traditional format, with questions by reporters.

5. A joint vice presidential/presidential debate on network television, with the pairs debating as teams—just as they run as teams.

6. A semifinal debate on network television between the presidential candidates, following a traditional format, with questions by reporters.

7. A final debate on network television, with the candidates asking the questions of each other, and structured to provide a direct exchange between the candidates.

All of these debates would be sponsored by a newly created National Endowment for Presidential Debates, which would choose the topics and select the questioners. Candidates of parties receiving federal election funds would be required to participate. The calendar on page 20 gives an example of what the debate schedule for the fall of 1992 might look like:

Possible Calendar for 1992

Date	Activity	Media
Jan.—June	Town Meetings	
	Issue Hearings	
	Issue Round-tables	
	Issue Debates	
April—June	Focus Groups	
August	Platform Defense	
Sept. 7	LABOR DAY	
Sept. 10	Kick-off Debate	Network, PBS, Cable
Sept. 15	Issue Conferences	PBS, Cable
Sept. 18	Issue Conferences	PBS, Cable
Sept. 21	Issue Conferences	PBS, Cable
Sept. 24	Issue Conferences	PBS, Cable
Sept. 29	Candidate/Staff Debate	Network, PBS, Cable
Oct. 2	Candidate/Staff Debate	PBS, Cable
Oct. 6	Candidate/Staff Debate	PBS, Cable
Oct. 9	V.P. Debate	Network, PBS, Cable
Oct. 14	Presidential/V.P. Debate	Network, PBS, Cable
Oct. 19	Semi-Final Debate	Network, PBS, Cable
Oct. 25	Final Debate	Network, PBS, Cable
Nov. 3	ELECTION DAY	

In addition to this intense fall schedule, the endowment would also sponsor a series of events during the winter, spring, and summer in preparation for the fall debates. These would include:

1. *Town meetings,* taking place from January through June in many parts of the country, to allow the public to express concerns about the major issues of the day and thereby develop an issues agenda to be debated in the fall. Portions of these would be taped and shown on cable and PBS.

2. *Issue hearings,* taking place from January through June, devoted to specific issues, at which experts and interested parties could testify. Portions of these would be taped and shown on cable and PBS.

3. *Issue conferences and debates* at which a selected group of ex-

perts and interested parties would discuss and debate the policy choices. A selected number of these would be taped and shown on cable and PBS.

4. *Solution focus groups* in which specific policy solutions to problems would be tested in a series of focus groups sponsored by the endowment.

5. *Platform defense forums* at which a designee of each candidate would be required to defend specific portions of his or her party's platform. This would force candidates to pay more attention to the platforms and would increase accountability.

Finally, the issue conference format would be used in the off-year election cycle to require the president and the leadership of the opposition party or parties to defend specific positions under cross-examination by experts. In this way, the president and congressional leadership would be held more accountable for their actions.

The aim is also to institute a series of predictable forensic encounters of similar format that would become as much a part of the election cycle as the New Hampshire primary or the conventions themselves. In this way, not only would candidates be given adequate opportunity to prepare for this exercise long in advance, but the rules of the game would no longer be part of the game itself.

This may seem like an ambitious agenda, but proposals for reform must meet the scope of the problem. No minor tinkering with the current system of debates will bring about the kind of fundamental changes that are needed in the campaign process. If we are to use the debate process to change the ambience of the campaign, to make the discussion of policy questions a central feature of the election season, and to force the candidates to pay attention to the kind of staff they will employ in their administration, then the practice of holding debates will have to become widespread, and the debates themselves will have to cover real substance. (The debates of the 1988 primary season have shown that merely holding large numbers of debates will not by itself force candidates to focus on issues.)

Some questions must be answered: Will the amplitude and intensity of the debate schedule proposed here be self-defeating? Is not the public already jaded by overexposure to the candidates? Will the menu prescribed here be appreciated mainly by the afficionados of C-Span and public television?

A lot, of course, will depend on the quality of the events and the level of discourse. There is certainly no evidence that the public is bored by quality programming dealing with public matters, especially issues that directly affect the viewer. And the whole point of these proposals is to have the public become more engaged. It is the restoration of content and immediacy that is the principal objective here.

Moreover, such a schedule of events will have the added benefits of (1) concentrating the energies and efforts of the candidates and their staffs on substantive issues, (2) forcing the media to alter the nature of their coverage, and (3) making the candidates play the role required of issue-oriented public servants seeking to educate the public about specific views on a broad range of issues. Ideas, not events, will dominate the process. An increasingly skeptical, if not cynical, public would quickly observe and honor these changes in our election format.

A lot of attention has been paid to the process of selecting presidential candidates, but not to the entire process of selecting a president. Yet the institutions we establish—both within and outside of the parties—play a decisive role in determining who becomes president. It is time we looked at this process in its totality, especially when we are recommending changes in parts of it.

Many observers have praised our current selection system, which begins in a formal sense nearly a year before the general election. They have commented on how it makes candidates meet people face-to-face on the farms of Iowa and in the hamlets of New Hampshire; how it forces candidates to hire or acquire the skills to run a large organization; how it tests their strategic and forensic skills; and how, through the need to raise money and position themselves with respect to other candidates, it forces them to define a relationship to constituencies.

The proposals contained in this report would add to this screening process by forcing candidates to defend their parties' platforms, set their agenda for the nation's future, demonstrate issues competence and the ability to devise solutions to the great questions of the day, recruit competent advisors in advance of the election, and stand up to the other candidates in direct forensic confrontation.

*   *   *

Taken as a whole, the proposals set forth here will provide voters with more information about the candidates and, perhaps most important, will create a system of accountability that makes our democracy more truly representative.

Moreover, the proposals will invite controversy. They will, no doubt, be attacked as too forbidding both because of their amplitude and because of the high standards they set. But the magnitude of the effort reflects the magnitude of the problem. To fulfill the exacting demands and awesome responsibilities of the most powerful office in the world, a rigorous and exacting set of requirements is precisely what America needs.

Chapter 4
The Proposal in Detail

A. The Events

1. Preconvention activity: preparation for the fall issue agenda

This proposal concerns itself entirely with the general election debates. The tradition of flexible primary debates between potential candidates of the two major parties that has developed in recent years should continue, with the parties, or the candidates, free to set their own agendas for the conduct of the debates. No recommendations, therefore, are made here about primary debates.

However, looking toward the debate schedule for the general election, it is important to create vehicles through which the public can become more involved, earlier, in defining the issues that will affect the platforms and the debates of the fall season.

Moreover, it is important that the parties and/or the candidates themselves begin to pay attention to hard policy questions earlier in the season. The disparity between attention paid to hard policy questions on the one side and mere public relations on the other is regrettably enormous.

To help identify public needs and areas of emerging public concern, to encourage more attention to policy choices during the campaign, to test public reaction to possible solutions to problems, and, not incidentally, to force campaigns to recruit the necessary staff to make possible serious policy discussions, the National Endowment would sponsor the following events during the period from January 1 to May 1:

a) "Town meeting" issue development

During the first four months of the election year, the endowment either would itself sponsor or would encourage and assist the parties to sponsor a large number of "town meetings," hearings devoted to issue development. These meetings would be held on the neighborhood level in front of representatives of the two major (or other qualifying) parties. The public would express its concerns about major issues and identify emerging problems. The "public" would be chosen by random sample to avoid "packing" by the candidates.

These meetings would take place in each state no less than one month before the primary or caucus held to select delegates to the national nominating conventions. Representatives of the candidates qualifying for federal matching funds would be invited to attend these town meetings.

The meetings would be presided over by a moderator, who would also serve as rapporteur; the moderator would have been selected by the endowment after consulting with local representatives of each party.

The rapporteur at each meeting would list the concerns brought up and, in consultation with the people present, would frame questions to the candidates about the problems aired. The topics and questions would be forwarded to:

    (1) the endowment to help plan questions for later phases of the debate process and

    (2) the various candidates and parties.

The candidates would then be asked to state their positions on the most important questions raised by the voters, as determined by the frequency with which each topic came up. The endowment would collect, publish, and publicize the availability of these compilations.

b) Issue hearings

Both political parties have experimented with platform hearings during the past decade. These have met with varying degrees of success because they have become tugs-of-war among factions within the parties. The National Endowment, as part of the process of developing questions for the debates and of involving the public in the development of issues, either could sponsor or could encourage others to sponsor issue hearings to which the interested public would be invited. Local not-for-profit interest groups in the cities selected for such hearings would be encouraged to cooperate in arranging attendance. The general public, of course, would also be eligible to attend.

These hearings would be set up in various regions of the country, beginning in January and lasting through May, inviting testimony from experts, interest groups, and the public at large. Each candidate would be asked to send a representative to testify or might wish to testify him or herself. Each hearing would be devoted to a specific topic, chosen by the endowment, and might go on for a week, depending on the number of individuals who wish to be heard. These sessions would be open, and the videotapes of them made available to the public. The testimony would be given to the issue staffs of the candidates and to the platform committees of the parties. In addition, a condensed version of each hearing—perhaps a half-hour in length— showing the highlights of the testimony and presenting all sides of the issue discussed would be prepared for airing on cable and PBS. The endowment would buy time to broadcast a selection of the most important of these hearing highlights and would fund publicizing both the hearings and the broadcasts.

c) "Solution" focus groups

During the past decade, public relations firms, survey research firms, and marketing firms have made extensive use of "focus groups" —random collections of individuals brought together to be sounded for their in-depth opinions on particular topics. They are used in politics both to find out about "sleeper" issues that might otherwise go unnoticed and to act as sounding boards to test voter reaction to campaign themes and even specific campaign advertising proposals.

The focus group can also be used for more substantive purposes: for example, to measure public reaction either to specific solutions to current problems or to the positions taken by the candidates on specific issues. The endowment would either sponsor or assist the parties to sponsor a series of focus groups for this purpose.

Tapes of these focus groups would be made available to the candidates, the parties, the media, and the public. Since the reactions of the participants might be very interesting to a wide television audience, the endowment could purchase time on cable and PBS to air a selection of such sessions.

Purpose: The major purpose of this preconvention activity is to change the ambience of the primary season by creating a climate in which the discussion of issues is more prominent. Greater public participation would mean wider involvement in the development of questions to be debated during the fall season. The hearings and focus group sessions would force candidates to pay more attention to public grievances and issues and to recruit staffs to deal with them. The solution focus groups would create opportunities for candidates to test voter reaction on a range of alternatives and would remind policy experts of the direct impact that public policy choices have upon individuals.

Needless to say, interest groups would be expected to play a major role in all of this. They are more likely to attend meetings and to testify than are ordinary citizens (which is one reason to include focus groups in the above menu of programs). Interest groups have the same right to be heard as anyone, but they tend to be better informed about the specifics of an issue than is the general public.

One purpose of this phase is precisely to provide a forum to interest groups. It is best that the "interest group" phase of the campaign be concentrated at the outset. If nothing else, this phase serves to identify these groups and the interests that they serve. As the campaign proceeds through the summer and into the fall, more national issues of general concern can be emphasized. In this way, the campaign, as the election nears, will move from narrower to broader concerns.

2. Platform defense

When the proposal outlined here becomes fully operational, the political party conventions would have to take place before August 15. The time between August 15 and Labor Day would be reserved for a period of "platform defense."

A series of two-hour sessions (in a "Meet the Press" or "Face the Nation" format) would be scheduled for each party, during which a representative of each candidate would be grilled (on camera) about specific provisions in the party platform by a panel of four people. The panel would include three experts in the policy area under discussion and one representative of the opposition party. If a candidate of a new party (or an independent) qualified, panels would be prepared for that candidate, and a fifth person would be included on the panels of the major-party candidates.

The designated representative would be responsible for expressing his or her candidate's views. Alternatively, the candidate might wish to attend some of these sessions personally. The sessions would be videotaped and shown on cable and PBS.

For purposes of platform defense, the country would be divided into five regions. Six two-hour sessions would be held in each region, for a total of sixty sessions for the two parties.

Each two-hour session might be devoted to several planks, including proposals of special regional relevance. Since there would not be a huge audience for these sessions, they would be broadcast only on cable (perhaps a few would be shown on PBS). However, the National Endowment would publicize them, especially to groups specially interested in each platform.

Depending on the topic, some of the sessions would be broadcast locally, some nationally. All would be on the public record, and all tapes would be available to each party to use in its advertising, thus holding the representatives accountable for the statements they made and the planks they defended.

Major-party participation would be required as a condition of federal financing for the general election campaign. New parties that met the financial requirements for participation in the fall debates before August 15 would be eligible to participate and would have to participate to receive matching funds.

Purpose: These sessions would force the parties to take their platforms more seriously and would force the candidates either to defend the party platform or to cite his or her differences with it. Moreover, candidates would have to develop serious issue-oriented staffs early in the campaign. And the sessions would provide the vehicle for continuing public participation in the agenda-setting process established during the spring months.

These sessions would also be, as a practical matter, a "college for interest groups," giving them an opportunity to grill representatives of the candidates on issues of direct concern to them.

The sixty sessions would also become screening sessions to assist the National Endowment in deciding who would be asked to appear as panelists at the national conferences and debates in the fall.

3. The "agenda-setting" kickoff debate

The formal campaign season would begin with a kickoff "agenda-setting" debate, held a few days after Labor Day, that would provide the candidates with the opportunity to set their fall campaign agendas.

This debate would last two hours and would be broadcast in prime time on network television. Each candidate would be given ten minutes for an opening statement and ten minutes for a closing statement, which could be used either to elaborate themes discussed in the convention acceptance speeches or to strike out in new directions.

Between the opening and closing statements, candidates would be questioned for about an hour by reporters. Answers would be limited to three minutes, with a two-minute rebuttal, for a total of about seven or eight questions for each candidate. The reporters would be allowed to ask follow-through questions on topics raised in the opening statements. Topics would be drawn from lists of issues submitted by each candidate in advance. In this way, each candidate could ensure that the important items on his or her campaign agenda would be covered.

If a third candidate qualifies, the debate would be lengthened by half an hour, with eight-minute opening and closing statements.

Purpose: It is important for the public to see the candidates in action and against each other early in the campaign. The experience of the Kennedy-Nixon and the Carter-Ford debates suggests that if public opinion is to have an opportunity to change—which is the whole reason for debates—it is important that people have an early view of the candidates. A debate at this time would give each candidate a national forum to set forth the grounds on which the campaign will be fought and would provide an opportunity to focus the messages set forth in the convention acceptance speech to a large national audience.

4. The issue conferences

The second phase of the campaign would consist of from four to six issue conferences. These would begin about a week after Labor Day and would continue for two or three weeks depending on the length of the campaign in a given year. Four are proposed for 1992 (see calendar, p. 20) because the election season that year is short (Labor Day is late and the election is early).

These conferences would consist of discussions between a candidate and his or her advisors and leading experts in a specific policy area.

They would be an hour to an hour and a half in length, followed immediately by an identical session with the other candidate. If three or more candidates qualified, then a third hour or a second set of conferences on another evening would be added. The order of appearance for the first conference would be determined by lot, followed by rotation in subsequent conferences.

To avoid overexposure, the conference debates would be broadcast on cable and PBS, although the networks could certainly cover them if they so desired.

Candidates would choose who they would bring along, but incumbents would be expected to bring cabinet officers or White House staff members (the national security advisor, members of the Council of Economic Advisors, science advisors, and other members of the administration). They would be entirely free to bring in other experts or more informal advisors.

Challengers would be expected to bring "shadow" cabinet advisors and others who they might eventually select as members of their administration. Although an appearance at the discussion would not be tantamount to an appointment, it would be reasonable to expect that some of the advisors would eventually serve in the government.

The "round table" format would allow the experts to grill the candidates (and their advisors) intensely, with both follow-through questions, direct comment on the answers, and rebuttal. Such a format would provide the opportunity for a free-flowing discussion of the issues. Each conference topic would be a specific policy area. With four to six of these conferences and three candidate/staff debates (see below) also devoted to different specific areas, policy alternatives would be discussed in a much more focused way than is possible in current presidential debates.

At least one issue conference or candidate/staff debate would be devoted to the administration of the federal government or the organization and control of the executive branch. (This would serve to educate not only the candidates but also the electorate.)

The panelists would not be the traditional reporters, but interested parties and experts in the field (academics and foreign and defense policy analysts, the president of the American Bar Association, leading civil and women's rights activists, representatives from the National League of Cities, representatives of organized labor, health-care specialists, and so on). In this way, a more substantive level of discussion would be possible.

Most of these panelists would have participated in the questioning during the earlier platform defense phase. On the basis of their performance during that phase (including their knowledge, their objectivity—or their valid representation of a point of view—and their ability to ask questions), they would be chosen by the National Endowment to participate in both the issue conferences and the candidate/staff debates. Each candidate would be given a list of prospective questioners in advance and would be given the right of preemptive challenge to a percentage of them.

The endowment would also develop a series of topics, based on issues raised during the preconvention phase as suggestions to the empaneled questioners. Topics might include: arms control; the Middle East; fiscal, monetary, and debt policy; the Japanese challenge; the farm problem; minority rights; the environment; policy toward Latin America; the Constitution and the judiciary; reform of the banking system; problems of the American city; science, technology, space, and research; energy and the environment; and health care and care for the elderly.

The topics for discussion and at least the general nature and outline of the questions would be shared with the candidates before the debate because total spontaneity on such important issues might give the impression of too casual or superficial an approach.

As a variant, the candidates could submit position papers in advance on the topic to be discussed. The interrogators would then frame the initial questions around the prepared statements.

If this format were chosen, candidates would be given ten minutes to set forth their general positions, followed by questions. The candidates would then be given five minutes to respond, either using all the time or relinquishing some to their advisors. A candidate who always relied on the experts would look ill informed; one who dominated the proceedings would look a little foolish.

After the response, follow-through questions and direct cross-examination of both candidates and their advisors would be permitted, creating the opportunity for an in-depth examination that would reveal how well the candidates grasp the issues. This procedure would also enable experts both to cross-examine the advisors and to plumb their basic assumptions.

Purpose: These issue conferences, which would be a new feature in the election campaign, would serve several purposes. The extensive media coverage they are likely to receive would have an enormous impact on the presidential election process. The media would be less inclined to analyze them to see "who won" and more inclined to analyze "whose policies make sense"—thus shifting their focus of campaign coverage away from the language of a sporting event and into the language of policymaking. They would raise the level of sophistication in which presidential debates are conducted and would provide, for the first time, in-depth examination of issues.

Even given an audience of just a few million, candidates could not afford to look foolish, ill prepared, or ill advised; viewers would include those who were most interested in, informed about, or affected by the topic under discussion. The impact of these debates would outweigh the size of the audience because a much larger portion of the audience is likely to be of the "swing" vote variety.

Candidates, knowing this, are not likely to miss the opportunity to perform well. Because they would have to bring experts to face the expertise of the questioners, they would have to recruit talented people or suffer from comparison with those who did. This substantive talent would help balance the influence of public relations experts in the campaign.

Furthermore, because they would pick advisors early in the campaign, the candidates and their advisors would be able to assess how well they could work together. Hugh Heclo has written eloquently about our "government of strangers," which he describes as the modern practice of assembling a government from people who have never worked together and who must therefore take time to get used to one another. This proposal would not eliminate the problem of unfamiliarity, but it would be a step in the right direction.

Equally important, the public would be given the opportunity to assess the quality of the staff being assembled by the candidate. Although technically we are electing a single person to be president (or president and vice president), a more realistic view of contemporary American politics suggests that we are actually selecting a team. In many ways, the quality of this team is almost as important as the quality of the president—and certainly is a reflection of it.

By bringing people with solid credentials into the center of public discussion early in the campaign, there is at least the chance that the level of public discourse will be raised. To be sure, "experts" vary in quality, and some may not resist the temptation to become showpeople, but this debate format will create the opportunity for serious issues to be discussed at a level of specificity not now achieved in any presidential campaign forum.

With the issue conferences and the issue-oriented candidate/staff debates scheduled at the rate of two per week during most of September and October, issues would dominate and would give the campaign a totally different ambience than it has today. Candidates would be forced to develop greater personal expertise, and the campaign itself would become more serious and more legitimate.

5. The candidate/staff debates

The third phase of the debate season, held during the first two weeks in October, would feature three (or four, depending on the calendar) staff-assisted candidate debates. These, unlike the issue conference "debates," would involve more direct confrontations, with both the candidates and their advisors present at the same time.

These debates would be two hours in length and would focus on a major foreign or domestic policy issue. The first, broadcast on network television during prime time, would actually be the second—the agenda-setting "kickoff" debate Labor Day week would also be covered by the networks—full-exposure debate for the presidential candidates. (The next two would be broadcast on PBS or on cable.) The endowment would choose the topic for the network debate.

If a third candidate qualified, the debates would be two and a half hours in length.

Topics debated in all of these candidate/staff debates would, however, be of the same level of specificity as those in the issue conferences. The panel asking the questions would be experts of the same type and caliber, chosen in the same way, and subject to preemptory challenge.

The candidates would again be asked to bring two or three of their policy experts, to participate in the debate. These advisors would be chosen from among those who participated in the issue conferences.

There would be a five-minute opening statement by each candidate. The panel of experts would then ask questions which either the candidate or his or her advisors would have five minutes to answer. (This is the same format that was proposed for the issue conference.)

Follow-through questions to either the candidate or the advisor would be permitted in each case, with two minutes for response. With two (or more) sets of candidates and advisors, however, no time would be available for commentary and rebuttal, as there was in the issue conference. Again, specific topics, or at least their general nature, would be submitted to the candidates one day in advance of the debate. The unrehearsed follow-through questions would, again, provide an important sense of a candidate's ability to think independently and would help gauge the depth of his or her true understanding.

In the last of these debates, the panel of experts would ask the initial question, but the follow-through questions would be asked by the opposition, the candidate, or at the direction of the candidate, one of the advisors. This would provide an opportunity for direct cross-examination to test the quality of the candidates.

Purpose: These debates would serve many of the same purposes as the issue conferences: they would force the candidates to have key advisors in place early; they would raise the level of discourse and add more sophistication to the discussion; and they would give issues more focus than is now the case. Also, they would help the voter evaluate the candidate's own level of expertise, and the level of dependence on advisors, as well as the quality of the advisors.

Going beyond the issue conference format, however, these issue debates would pit the candidates and their advisors directly against each other. The more open format of the final debate would enable the public to see at one time both sets of advisors and to evaluate their ability to stand up to each other under substantive cross-examination.

6. The vice presidential debate

With vice presidential debates having been held in 1976 and in 1984, a tenuous tradition of holding them exists. This proposal calls for the candidates to debate each other before network television. The questioning by the media should be general, with no restrictions on the topics.

The debate would last for two hours. Each candidate would be given six minutes for an opening statement, followed by an hour of questions by journalists in a traditional format, with each candidate then having three minutes to answer.

During the remainder of the time, the candidates would be given the opportunity to ask each other questions. Thirty seconds would be allotted to ask the question, two minutes to respond. The questioning would rotate.

If more than two candidates qualified, the debate would last two and a half hours.

This vice presidential debate would be the first of four network debates in the course of the two and a half weeks that would end the debate season. Moreover, it would set the stage for the presidential/vice presidential debate and would culminate in the two presidential debates.

Purpose: Again, the purpose would be to acquaint voters with the qualifications of the vice presidential candidates, which, in turn, reflects upon the judgment of those who choose them. The purpose of the direct questioning format during the second half of the debate would be to sharpen the contrasts between the two candidates. If more than two candidates qualified, then an appropriate format would be designed to permit debate among them. The direct question format, however, would be preserved.

7. The presidential/vice presidential debate

The next debate would be one in which the presidential and the vice presidential candidates would appear together. This is another new feature of this debate proposal.

The sequence of network debates would be the agenda-setting kickoff debate, the two-hour issue debate between the presidential candidates, the vice presidential debate, then the combined presidential/vice presidential debate. These would be followed by two final presidential debates, for a total of six network debates. This is not substantially more than the four we have had in the past.

In the proposed sequence, the presidential candidates open and close the debate season; the two debates that involve the vice presidential candidates are in the middle. This gives a proper balance to the importance of the vice president as the clearly subordinate figure. It is also preferable, however, for the vice presidential candidates to appear alone first, by way of introduction to the voters, and then with their presidential candidates. The last memory of their network performance should be that of a team—which is, after all, what people vote for on a ticket.

The joint debate would be shorter, lasting only one hour and a half. The presidential candidate would be given four minutes for an opening statement, followed by a three-minute opening statement by his or her running mate. Then the opposition candidates would be given their four-minute and three-minute equivalent.

For the rest of the debate, each team would be given a combined four minutes to answer a question. The questions would come from senior journalists and could cover all issues, both domestic and foreign. They would be addressed to the presidential candidates, who would take as much of the four minutes as they wished and would then ask the vice presidential candidates if they had anything to add. The presidential candidates could take all the time, or none of it, but would as a matter of course share it with their running mate. (A candidate would look foolish hogging all the time, or deferring all the time.)

Each presidential and vice presidential team would share eight minutes apiece for closing statements, dividing the time as they wished, with the vice presidential candidate going first in each case.

Purpose: This debate would enable the voter to see each set of presidential and vice presidential candidates operate as a team: they run as a ticket and should therefore appear at least once together. The debate would also give the vice presidential candidates additional exposure.

8. Semi-final debate
The semifinal debate would most resemble the debates of recent history. It would take place on the Monday or Tuesday two weeks before the election. (See calendar, p. 20.) It would be two hours in length, like the kickoff debate. Each candidate would be allowed ten minutes for an opening statement, followed by questions from a panel of reporters. The first forty minutes of questions would be on domestic policy, the second forty on foreign policy. Each candidate would be given ten minutes for a closing statement.

If a third candidate qualifies, the debate would last two and a half hours.

Again, these are long opening and closing statements, but the candidates then have the opportunity to include real *content* in their prepared statements, thus discouraging glib one-line presentations of positions. Candidates might still be glib, but at least they will not be forced to be so by the format.

Purpose: This debate, designed to fulfill the traditional role that debates have served to date—an expanded joint press conference—reverts to the format of journalists as questioners.

By the end of this debate, journalists would have served as questioners in the kickoff debate (although with restrictions on the topics, as discussed above), in the first half of the vice presidential debate, in the combined presidential/vice presidential debate, and in this semifinal debate. They would have participated in four debates, all of which would receive network coverage. This degree of participation seems adequate to preserve the traditional role of journalists in the debate sequence. That role is an expression of our belief that a free press is an important element in the democratic process.

The press will have the opportunity to ask about issues and policy choices as well as about other aspects of the campaign that would not be covered in the issue conferences and the issue debates. The age, experience, and other personal qualifications of the candidates, for example, might come up, as might questions about the dynamics of the campaign, about generalized visions for the future of the country, about honesty in government, about character, and so on. Although such topics may have received disproportionate attention in recent campaigns, we should avoid the temptation to allow the pendulum to swing too far in the opposite direction. Such questions have their place, and these debates will provide the occasion for their asking.

9. The final debate

The final debate would take place on the Sunday evening nine days before the election. Voters would therefore have the time necessary to digest the results. The final week should be devoted to traditional campaigning and advertising, as the candidates themselves decide.

The final debate would be one and a half hours long. (If there are three qualifying candidates, it would be two hours.) For near-total coverage, it would be broadcast on network television, PBS, and cable.

No panel of reporters would ask questions; a moderator would be present to introduce the candidates and to monitor the time. The candidates would question each other.

The debate would consist of a twelve-minute opening statement by each candidate, time enough to develop themes and present a message. Apart from paid advertising, it would be the candidates' final network-covered statements. Shorter presentations simply do not allow the themes of the campaign to be adequately summarized.

After the opening statements are presented, the first candidate, previously selected by lot, would address a question to the opponent. The questions would be limited to one minute in length. The opponent would have three minutes to answer; the first candidate would then have one minute to respond and to pose a follow-through question. The other candidate would have two minutes for a reply to this follow-through question.

Then the second candidate would ask a question of the first, followed by a commentary and follow-through, and so on back and forth.

Time would be left so that each candidate would have an eight-minute closing statement.

No restrictions would be placed on the topics of the questions.

Purpose: This debate format would show the ability of each candidate to stand alone against the other, and to raise questions he or she might want brought up. It would permit cross-examination of each others' policies. The one-on-one format, a dramatic and fitting climax to the debate season, would become an important tradition in American politics.

10. The off-year biennial issue conferences

In the British parliamentary tradition, the government in power is subject to repeated cross-examinations on its policies. The cross-examination is conducted in several ways: through question time, through the annual debate on the Speech from the throne, through major debates on proposed legislation, and, most important, through debates on resolutions of confidence.

Cabinet members are subject to cross-examination by their shadow opposite, and if the topic under discussion is sufficiently important, the prime minister will conclude the debate, defending the cabinet's policies in a sharp exchange with the opposition. Similar institutions exist in Canada and in most other democracies.

The American system has no effective counterpart to this practice. And events of the past two decades suggest that a forum is needed in which the president is obliged to defend the policies of his administration in a public and adversarial situation, akin to that which takes place in Parliament.

Such a defense should not necessarily take place with great frequency, certainly not so often as in Britain and elsewhere. But it does seem that the president (or the successor for a lame duck) should be asked to defend the policies of the government in detailed fashion at least once every two years.

The schedule of debates outlined above would certainly ensure that a president running for reelection would be obliged to defend his administration's policies at the end of the first term. This schedule would also ensure that representatives of the president's own party would fulfill this role in the last year of the president's term, should that president be a lame duck or choose not to run again. (A sitting president should be given the option of designating a spokesperson of his or her choice.)

Once every four years, however, is not sufficient.

Under this proposal, the president would be obliged, during the fall of the off-year congressional elections, to hold a series of issue conferences like those outlined above, during which cross-examination would take place.

Six issue conferences would be scheduled during September of the off-year congressional elections. These would cover major areas of foreign policy, defense, the economy, social welfare, human rights, and perhaps national goals. The topics would be less specific than those for the issue conferences in the presidential election year.

The off-year issue conferences would last an hour and a half. The president and two or three of his key advisors would be examined by a panel of four policy experts and one member of the opposition party. The panel would be chosen by the endowment (as for the issue conferences) from individuals who had taken part in the previous election cycle. Again, the president and advisors would be given the right of preemptory challenge to a percentage of the questioners. If a new party had qualified for federal matching funds at the previous presidential election, then it would also have a representative on each panel, for a total of six.

The format would be similar to that of the issue conferences discussed above, with questions directed both to the candidate and to the advisors, with adequate follow-through questions and open exchanges.

The opposition parties, to receive federal funds at the subsequent general election, would also have to participate in an issue conference. The national committee of each qualifying party would nominate a representative to be cross-examined on one of the six areas that would be negotiated by the endowment with the parties involved.

Purpose: The purpose of this proposal, quite simply, is to raise the level of accountability of the president to the electorate.

11. State of the Union responses
The networks have customarily permitted members of the opposition party to respond to the president's State of the Union address. These

responses have, however, been of uneven quality and have certainly lacked the forensic majesty of the State of the Union address.

Given that the State of the Union address is a constitutionally mandated duty of the president and that it is *supposed* to be an act of national leadership rather than partisan politics, it would be inappropriate to create an identical forum (say, another joint session of Congress) for the opposition to respond. However, an annual issue debate at the opening of a new session of Congress might be considered.

Under this proposal, the endowment would sponsor a response to the State of the Union speech, one week later, to be delivered as a formal speech to an appropriate audience (for example, members of Congress, governors, and mayors, in a suitable hall, not necessarily in Washington) by a single chosen representative of the opposition party.

Four representatives, plus alternates, might be chosen, one to present the response for the next four years, at the party's quadrennial presidential nominating convention. Each party would prepare the list in the event that it does not win the presidency.

If more than one opposition party were eligible, other speeches would be permitted.

In addition to the formal speeches, the endowment would sponsor a two-hour "Legislative Priorities" program during January on network television, in which the congressional leadership of each party would be given the opportunity to set forth its legislative agenda for the coming session of Congress.

Purpose: Again, this proposal would further national debate on the issues of the day and would use the forensic advantages of the adversarial process to hold elected officials more fully accountable to the public.

B. Participation

Nothing in this proposal precludes candidates from engaging in as many other debates as they wish. However, to achieve the objectives set forth in this proposal, participation by the nominees of the major parties in the National Endowment debates must be mandatory. If not, even a threat of boycott by a candidate who does not need the exposure will give that candidate enough leverage to alter the rules, substitute other debates, and undercut the process.

Constitutionally, the only way to make participation mandatory (as a practical matter) is to make receipt of federal financing conditional upon participation in this series of debates. This would require legislation and clarification of terms.

1. Major parties

A major party is defined under the campaign finance laws as a party whose candidate for president received 25 percent of the popular vote at the previous general election.

The candidates of the major parties would be eligible and required to participate in the debate schedule because receipt of federal funds by that party and its candidate for the campaign would be conditional on it.[1]

Receipt of federal funds would also be conditional on participation in the previous off-year round of issue conferences: by the president in the case of the party that occupies the White House and by the congressional leadership in the case of the major party not occupying the White House.

Receipt of federal funds would also be conditional on participation in the platform defense.

The major parties would be guaranteed appropriate opportunity to participate in the State of the Union responses.

2. Independent candidates and parties that have not achieved major-party status

a) Candidates other than those of the major parties would be eligible to participate in the fall debate schedule if they met all of the following criteria:

(1) They had achieved ballot status in enough states to create an electoral college mathematical majority by September 1 of the election year.

(2) They had received a minimum of 15 percent support in at least three of six presidential trial-heat polls, head to head with the candidates of the major parties, conducted between August 15 and September 1, by six nationally recognized independent polling firms or university consortia commissioned by the endowment upon petition by the candidate or the candidate's party no later than August 1 of the election year. The endowment would be responsible for sample design and questionnaire design.

(3)They had either:

(a) Received 5 percent or more of the popular vote at the previous general election (thus qualifying them for prospective federal funds); or:

(b) Raised by August 15 an amount of money equal to the total amount of money that they would be eligible to receive in federal funds by achieving 5 percent of the total popular vote in the election the following November (this amount changes from election to election, but it is in excess of $4 million) with a minimum of $50,000 in each of twenty states in amounts of $250 or less (which is precisely ten times the eligibility requirement for federal matching funds for the primary season).*

(4) They had produced a platform stating their positions on the major issues of the day, and had fully participated in the platform defense program along with the major-party candidates. Eligibility to participate would be contingent on meeting one of the criteria set forth in section 3 above. This might mean that some candidates would participate in the platform defense portion of the schedule but not in the fall debates if, for example, they subsequently failed to meet the ballot access requirements or failed to get 15 percent in three of six polls. There would certainly be no harm in this, and their participation would be a creative addition to the general national discussion to have a wider range of policy proposals set forth and defended (and carried on PBS and cable). The reason that this is set forth as a requirement is so that the nonmajor party candidates could not escape defending their platforms.

Also, nonparty candidates, like major party candidates, would be *required* to participate in the fall debate schedule as a condition for receiving federal funding.

b) Independent candidates or parties that had acquired eligibility to participate in the fall debate schedule would also be permitted to join the issue conferences during the following off-year election cycle. If they received 5 percent of the vote in the general election, and wished

---

* If a candidate did not meet this eligibility criterion by August 15, the endowment would not be required to conduct the polls described in section 2 above.

to receive the federal funds they would thus be entitled to, then they would *have to* participate in the issue conferences (in which they would be subject to cross-examination by experts in the field) held during the off-year elections.

c) Independent candidates or parties that were eligible to participate in the fall presidential-election-year debate schedule and who achieved 15 percent of the total popular vote in the election would be permitted (but not mandated) to participate in the responses to the State of the Union address for the next four years. This more stringent requirement to achieve State of the Union response status is to ensure participation only by serious opposition in these formal events.

C. Sponsorship and Implementation:
The National Endowment for Presidential Debates

Sponsorship for presidential debates in the past has been an issue of some controversy.[2] The need for a sponsor has involved the "fairness doctrine" and the designation of the debates as "news events." To circumvent the problem, the League of Women Voters has itself sponsored several debates in the past, thus enabling the networks to cover them as "news events." Recently, the parties themselves set up a joint commission to sponsor the debates.

Having the major parties sponsor the debates creates problems of its own, especially the problem of participation by legitimate new-party efforts and independent candidates. Instead, there is a need for an independent umpire, and that need cannot be fully served by the League of Women Voters or by any other private organization. The umpire must be able to set the rules and to structure events unfettered by candidate threats to refuse to participate. By making federal funding contingent on participation, these threats will become meaningless. In addition, it would prevent extensive haggling over the rules from year to year—which tends to delegitimize the process.

Moreover, the ambitious schedule set forth in this proposal involves the extensive recruitment of questioners, selection of topics, purchase of significant amounts of broadcast time, and the development of fair ground rules. It requires a small, permanent staff reporting to an impartial group of overseers or trustees.

It is to achieve these objectives that we have proposed that Congress create a National Endowment for Presidential Debates.

In proposing to create a National Endowment for Presidential Debates, I am well aware that it involves a voyage between Scylla (preserving accountability to our elected representatives in Congress) and Charybdis (keeping it free of political influence).

As a member of Congress for twenty years, I fully appreciate its belief that it is the constitutional protector of the electoral process. Congress jealously guards that right. The battle over the creation of the Federal Election Commission, after all, went all the way to the Supreme Court because of a congressional desire to make appointments to that commission.

Furthermore, there is some residual hostility to an agency or bureaucracy coming between the legislative branch and the voters. Even though this proposal relates to elections involving the executive branch, the principle is nevertheless deeply rooted in congressional minds.

The other caveat is that unless the endowment is free from any shadow of political influence, not only would it fall prey to partisan infighting and gamesmanship, but it would also erode the legitimacy of the whole election process.

The following details are offered to meet the challenge of providing a reasonable degree of congressional oversight (without which such an endowment could not be created in the first place), as well as a reasonable degree of autonomy. Both are necessary for the process to remain legitimate in the eyes of the public.

In effect, this proposal calls for broad participation by many different people, interest groups, and power centers (including Congress) in the creation of the endowment, and an equitable mixture of both public and private funding to provide a balance between accountability and independence after its creation.

To make the endowment work, a consensual process must attend its creation. While each party may have its presidential and congressional wings, as a practical matter Congress will not enact the enabling legislation unless there is both public endorsement of it and presidential party concurrence. The process of defining the structure and duties of the endowment, therefore, becomes almost as important as its ultimate purpose.

Fortunately, we have a good analogue in the Corporation for Public Broadcasting. Before it was created by Congress, the groundwork had been prepared by the report of the Carnegie Foundation that recommended the ground rules for its composition, the selection process for its directors, and the nature and sources of its funding.

The issues involved in creating a National Endowment for Presidential Debates are similar, but more politically sensitive, and involve some of the most powerful people in the country in ways that will directly affect their political power and prestige. The endowment must be set up far enough in advance of the next presidential election so that concern by individual candidates for the tactical advantages of the moment will not sabotage the process or warp its objectives. The structure and the rules, therefore, should be in place long before the candidates are—and this means that legislation setting up the endowment should be enacted by the 101st Congress. It would, therefore, make sense for the 101st Congress to create a Presidential/Congressional Commission early in 1989 to be appointed by the incoming president, and confirmed by the Senate, to make recommendations for the creation of an endowment and report back within the year. The commission should include perhaps a dozen people— Democrats, Republicans, and Independents. It should be drawn from former presidential and vice presidential candidates, former party leaders, and prestigious individuals no longer active in politics whose presence will lend legitimacy to the process.

This commission should be mandated to seek input from a variety of key people, including current and potential candidates, active party leaders, key congressional figures, and representatives of interest groups and of the media. Private organizations, such as foundations with long records of public service, and academics who are experts on the political process might also be consulted.

The commission should report to the president and to the Congress no later than January 1, 1990 (the start of the second session of the 101st Congress), so that enabling legislation can be enacted by the end of that Congress. This would give the endowment a full year to organize before the 1992 election cycle begins in earnest in January of 1992.

The appointment of a presidential commission would first be authorized by Congress, giving Congress input from the initial stage.

As a practical matter, Congress acts only when it is responding to some perceived pressure from its constituents. New proposals must sail on a wind of some public demand. The Federal Election Commission and the presidential campaign financing law, for example, were responses to Watergate. Those of us in Congress who had supported reform before Watergate were able to use the public clamor arising from that unfortunate episode to convince skeptical colleagues of the need for reform.

At the moment, we have no Watergate, but we do have widespread public skepticism about the process by which we select our president, and we do have widespread support for a more reasoned discussion of the issues in a presidential campaign.

There is academic support, and there is powerful "private" interest that might be expected to support such moves for reform, namely, the media. Although this debate proposal is aimed at correcting abuses by the media, the increased schedule of debates and their different formats would create new opportunities for coverage and therefore might extend (as well as reform) the role of the media in elections.

Furthermore, the proposals for institutionalizing the State of the Union responses and for requiring the president to defend his or her policies at least once every two years in a formal setting would command solid support in Congress (which often feels frustrated by the ability of presidents to hide behind privilege and prerogatives and to avoid the difficult questions that Congress wants answered). Support would likely be bipartisan, as long as the provisions were designed to come into force far enough in the future.

There are, therefore, good reasons to believe that these proposals could realistically come into practice.

Although a presidential commission should be the forum for developing the endowment idea and giving it concrete form, it is appropriate here to at least make some preliminary suggestions about its organization and funding.

It is proposed that the National Endowment for Presidential Debates be run by a Board of Trustees, which would, in turn, be responsible for the recruitment of a small permanent staff (supplemented by temporary help during the last year of an election cycle).

The duties of the trustees would be to select the staff, disburse funds, serve as a final board of review, and settle any disputes that might arise. The trustees and staff would determine the eligibility of parties and candidates to participate in the debates, establish the ground rules (in consultation with the participants), make the arrangements, select the topics for the issue conferences and issue debates (subject to peremptory challenges as outlined earlier), recruit the questioners, buy the media time, arrange publicity, and certify participation to the Federal Election Commission.

1. The trustees

A board of fifteen trustees would be appointed by the president and confirmed by the Senate. They would have staggered five-year terms. (At the beginning, the new trustees would have terms from one to five years to create the schedule of staggered terms.) By statute, no more than seven could be from the same political party. The model for this would be the Corporation for Public Broadcasting.

The endowment would be set up as an independent agency with independent sources of income, as detailed below, to separate it from both presidential and congressional political pressures associated with the appropriations process.

The trustees might be citizens deemed "beyond ambition," such as former presidents, vice presidents, or one-time candidates for those jobs, or others with distinguished records of public service, including persons from the electronic and print media.

2. The staff

The permanent staff would consist of a director, treasurer, general counsel, and such additional personnel as needed to implement the decisions of the Board of Trustees, all subject to strict control by the board.

The organizational structure of the endowment would be kept simple and nonhierarchical. The treasurer, general counsel, and staff director would report directly to the trustees. As a public corporation, and not a government agency, the endowment would be exempt from the civil service classification system. The fund-raising operation would be permitted to be as large as its own successes justified.

3. Duties

a) Determining eligibility

The first responsibility of the endowment (handled by its office of general counsel) would be to establish the eligibility of the parties and their candidates to participate. They would receive Federal Election Commission certification of a party's major-party status. In the case of nonmajor parties, they would receive and verify documents certifying ballot access, receive commission certification that the fund-raising requirements had been met, determine compliance with the platform defense provisions of eligibility, and commission the polls upon receipt of petition for debate participation. The commission would be mandated to comply with the appropriate requests of the endowment. With respect to the polls:

• The survey research firms or university consortia selected would be expected to be firms not engaged in political polling during the same election cycle.

• The endowment would specify the size and dimensions of the sample, including any screening questions to filter out people not eligible to vote. It would be expected that the sample size for each national survey would be at least 1,200.

• The endowment would specify the questionnaire design. This would include not only the precise determination of the trial heats to determine candidate eligibility, but also questions to determine what are the pressing issues of the day to assist the endowment in determining the topics for the issue conferences and issue debates.

• The endowment would specify the precise eligibility requirement. It is recommended that this be 15 percent of the total of the stated preferences for the major party candidates plus the stated preferences for the candidate(s) petitioning for eligibility, and that it not include undecided voters.

b) Establishing ground rules

The endowment would determine the ground rules for the different types of debates: overall length, length of opening and closing statements, time allotted to respond to questions, types of follow-through questions and comments permitted, and so on. It would have to establish a fair rule of procedure for determining the order of appearance and questioning.

The endowment should be made subject to all of the applicable provisions of the Administrative Procedures Act, which requires notice, hearings, and publication for comment by interested parties. There is, in short, no intention to vest vast discretionary powers in the endowment without appropriate safeguards.

c) Arrangements

The endowment would, in consultation with the participants, select the dates and sites for the debates. The candidates would not have to be in the same cities for the issues conferences if different sets of panelists were used to ask the questions of each team. Although it is technically possible for a debate to take place with the principals in different locations (one of the Kennedy-Nixon debates took place with the candidates in different studios in different cities), the joint-appearance debate is by far the best. The schedule as set forth (including full candidate/staff debates and regular debates, but not issue conferences) would require six joint appearances by the presidential candidates, one by the vice presidential candidates, and one where both the presidential and vice presidential candidates would appear. Such a schedule, taking place over about two months, should not create undue logistical problems for candidate scheduling operations.

d) Selection of debate topics

It would be the responsibility of the endowment to determine:

• The topics for the issue hearings, the issue debates, and the "solution" focus groups during the preconvention phase. In selecting the admittedly limited number of topics to be considered, the endowment could draw upon the following sources for topic ideas: the town meeting issue development forums, suggestions from the parties and the public, traditional planks in party platforms, and its own survey research. The endowment should also consult with representatives of the candidates.

The trustees would be expected to be directly involved with topic selection. Again, the principle of limited peremptory challenge would be part of this process. The number of challenges would be carefully explored by the board, and the details would be spelled out under rules adopted only after due notice, hearings, and publication for comment.

• In determining the topics for discussion in the issue conferences and in the candidate/staff debates, the endowment would be expected to draw upon the same sources as for the preconvention schedule, plus the topics developed in the course of the preconvention schedule itself. Again, limited peremptory challenges would be permitted.

e) Selection of questioners

The proposal envisions three basic types of questioners: (1) journalists; (2) experts, including specialty journalists, academics, consultants, former government officials, heads of professional organizations; and (3) the candidates themselves.

The preconvention schedule and the platform defense schedule would, among other purposes, help identify qualified people to do the questioning during the fall schedule. There would be many forums during which literally hundreds of people would be asking questions. These would be videotaped, and the endowment staff, together with the parties and the candidates, would have the opportunity to review the forensic abilities and general competence of the questioners and would select from among them.

As a matter of fairness, the candidates should be given a *limited* right of peremptory challenge. They could base their decisions on the videotapes of the earlier performances, among other criteria.

The journalists in the fall would be selected from among the prominent journalists of the day, as has been the custom in past presidential debates. Again, the participants would be given a *limited* peremptory challenge privilege.

The original selection of expert questioners for the preconvention period would be made by the endowment staff from traditional sources of professional expertise: contributors to journals, officials of professional societies, published authors, and other prominent people with specific expertise.

f) Purchase of media time

The endowment would be empowered to purchase media time on cable and PBS for the preconvention schedule and the platform defense hearings. It would also be empowered to purchase time for the fall schedule of issue conferences and debates. The networks, while paid for the time, would be required to make time available for the full schedule of network debates set forth in this proposal.

With respect to the issue conferences and nonnetwork fall events, PBS would be required to carry all of them. Cable stations would not be required to do so, but the endowment would have ample funds available to purchase a large amount of cable time.

g) Publicity

In addition to scheduling the events, the endowment would be expected to publicize them. The major network debates in the fall would receive much publicity from the networks themselves. But other events would need to be well publicized by the endowment to generate a large enough audience to fulfill the missions intended for them.

Two basic kinds of publicity are indicated: general publicity in the television media preceding the event and specialized publicity to those groups whom the endowment would regard as especially interested parties. For example, an issue conference on care for the elderly would receive targeted publicity to senior citizens and organizations involved with their welfare.

h) Certification

The endowment would certify to the Federal Election Commission that the candidates had complied with the requirements set forth so that campaign funds could be released. To ensure compliance, funds would be released throughout the season; the last 20 percent of the federal allotment—some $10 million—would not be released until after completion of the final debate. This coincides with the amount of money usually spent in the last ten days of the campaign.

4. Finance

For the initial election cycle, the endowment would be funded by Congress, although from the very beginning it would be permitted to engage in its own fund-raising activities. Nonpublic funds would be spent by the endowment at the discretion of the trustees but only for purposes authorized in the enabling legislation. They would be kept separate from the congressional appropriations process.

The endowment would not receive money through the federal appropriation process after the initial election cycle. There would be four continuing sources of funds:

a) Tax-deductible contributions from the public and from charitable foundations. These would be used primarily to supplement its preconvention schedule of town meetings, solution focus groups, and other educational programs. A permanent fund-raising staff would serve as the recruitment vehicle to raise these funds. Many not-for-profit groups might well wish to underwrite specific preconvention activities of interest to their members. In furthering its fund-raising activities, the endowment would be permitted to engage in public appeals. It might expect the networks to provide it with some free time for public service fund-raising advertising.

b) Grants, especially for those televised debates not carried free by the networks, from sponsors, whose sponsorship would be acknowledged before the debate, as the Corporation for Public Broadcasting now does for many of its programs: "The following program is made possible by a grant from. . . ." Considering the audience for presidential debates, there should be little difficulty in raising money from this source.

c) A special fund that would be established to receive money from the surplus in the current "check-off" system on the income tax form, in the same way that money for campaign financing is now raised. The money would go directly to the endowment, to be used at the discretion of the trustees.

d) Congressional appropriations. Although large amounts of money would not be required, the proposal has purposely not shied away from the congressional appropriation process altogether. The proposals for financing the endowment have been deliberately structured to ensure that congressional oversight can provide the necessary checks and balances. This provision is needed to enhance congressional receptivity for the idea of an endowment.

However, after the first election the endowment, I hope, would operate independently of the appropriations process and would be truly an impartial umpire of presidential debates. (The Corporation for Public Broadcasting has traditionally received most of its funding from private sources.[3])

5. Budget
The annual cost of the permanent staff, permanent staff support, office

space, and other general services, together with the State of the Union responses, should not exceed $2.5 million. For three out of four years, this should be fully adequate to run the endowment. The federal income tax check-off system, as extended for this purpose, should be more than adequate to meet this annual expenditure. Given the level of response to the current check-off system, an estimated $5 million per year could be expected to come from this source, half of which would be banked for election-year expenditures. The election-year expenditures, of course, will be much higher:

a) The pre-Labor Day event expenditures (for town meetings, issue hearings, issue conferences and debates, solution focus groups, and platform defense sessions) would be paid for out of money raised by the endowment fund-raisers from tax-deductible contributions from the public and from charitable foundations. The extent of these programs would be determined by the amount of money raised by the fund-raisers. Again, in the first election cycle, congressional appropriations could be used as seed money to initiate these programs.

b) The fall debate schedule would be funded out of revenues put aside from the check-off system, from debate sponsorship, and from direct appeals to the viewers. The principal expenditures here would be for logistic support (renting studios, etc.), publicity, and air time. Only a small token payment would be given to the questioners, although their expenses would have to be met. As a preliminary working estimate—and this is an area which the commission will have to explore further—$25 million above and beyond normal annual endowment expenditures appears to be an adequate sum in an election year. It would be broken down as follows: $5 million for logistical support and $20 million for publicity and air time. Twice this sum would be a small price to pay for strengthening our democracy, but twice this sum would almost certainly involve substantial appropriated funds. The joinder of both public and private financing that we have proposed will safeguard the process against undue political influence while assuring Congress that oversight has not been abandoned and that the endowment can be held accountable.

It is expected that the nationally televised candidate-on-candidate debates would be carried *gratis* by the networks as news events and as is now done on PBS. The networks also can be expected to give these debates adequate publicity.

In addition, however, the networks, cable, and PBS would be compensated for carrying the issue conferences and candidate/staff debates they are expected to carry, and the endowment would be responsible for publicizing them. For this, the $20 million seems adequate.

This amount can come from three sources: monies banked from the check-off system ($8 million, including interest), foundations and acknowledged debate sponsors ($10 million), and the net from direct appeals to the voters ($2 million).

Needless to say, the funding process is one that the Presidential/Congressional Commission will give close attention to, as it explores alternative sources. The point, however, is that adequate independent funding for such a debate program seems well within the reach of the endowment.

Notes

Chapter 1

1. These different forms of representation have been recognized by many scholars, most notably Hannah Pitkin and Heinz Eulau. See Hannah Pitkin, *The Concept of Representation* (Berkeley: 1967). See also, John Wahlke, Heinz Eulau, William Buchanan, and LeRoy Furgeson, *The Legislative System* (New York: 1962).

2. Evron Kirkpatrick says that "purists" who want mandatory debates really want "responsible" parties ("Presidential Candidate 'Debates': What Can We Learn from 1960?" in Austin Ranney, *The Past and Future of Presidential Debates* [American Enterprise Institute, Washington, D.C.: 1980], p. 44); but surely one may be permitted a more modest objective: responsible candidates.

3. Walter Lippmann, *Public Opinion* (New York: 1982).

4. Theodore S. White, *The Making of the President 1972* (New York: Bantam, 1973), p. 327.

5. See John Corry, "In the Debates, Appearance Conquers Substance," *The New York Times,* January 24, 1988.

6. P. E. Converse, "Information Flow and the Stability of Partisan Attitudes," in A. Campbell et al., *Elections and the Political Order* (New York: 1966).

Chapter 2

1. Among those who have looked at the question of how the process as a whole affects the outcome are journalists, such as David Broder; academics, such as Ted Lowi; and people with government experience, such as Lloyd Cutler.

2. See Alan Stone: "And while an American election provides a vehicle to help resolve differences among interest groups or to declare victors among candidates, it is certainly not useful to consider issues seriously," in Thomas Ferguson and Joel Rogers, *The Hidden Election: Politics and Economics in the 1980 Presidential Campaign* (New York: 1981).

Chapter 4

1. Because no one is constitutionally required to speak—as a technicality, participation would be defined as appearing on the platform for the duration of the debate. A candidate, presumably, would have the right to refuse to answer questions, and the voters would be able to draw any inferences they wished from this refusal.

2. And still is. See Margaret Carlson, "The Fight to Run the '88 Debates," *Channels,* November 1986, pp. 46-47.

3. Bernevia McCalip, "Public Broadcast Funding: The Process and Current Issues," Congressional Research Service, April 22, 1986.

Index